Also by Dr. Cheri L. Florance:

- *BE ME: Brain Engineering of My Emotions*, in press, Brain Science Publishing, 2009

- *Autism: A New Hope—Unlocking The Mysteries Of The Maverick Mind*, Brain Science Publishing, 2009

- *The Maverick Mind,* Penguin Books, 2004

- *A Boy Beyond Reach,* Simon & Schuster, 2004

- *Stutter-Free Speech*, Charles E. Merrill Publishing, 1980

AMP Up With The Animals

AMPlify Attention-Memory-Processing

A program designed to help parents and their children build an integrated brain engineering circuit for efficient and effective thinking and communication.

By

Cheri L. Florance, Ph.D.

Brain Engineering Labs
New York, NY
www.cheriflorance.com
braindr@cheriflorance.com

ISBN-13: 978-0-578-02959-7

Dear Reader,

AMP Up—Amplifying Your Attention, Memory & Processing—is a program designed to build an integrated brain engineering circuit for efficient and effective thinking and communication. You will learn how to improve the brain's ability to manage knowledge visually, verbally, or bi-modally.

The "AMP Up" program grew out of my many years as a brain scientist, therapist, and clinical researcher. However, my scientific credentials didn't prepare me for the birth of my third child. Even as an infant, Whitney did not connect with me in the same way as my other two children. His problem was so severe that I could shout in his ear and he wouldn't respond. He seemed not to feel pain, and didn't recognize members of his family as people. Whitney was eventually labeled autistic and given an I.Q. of 46.

I was devastated. However, I began to see the visual genius in his everyday behavior, which led me to believe he could be reached. Gradually, Whitney "taught" me how to use his Visual Coders to create a brain architecture for language, and by the time he was in high school, his language abilities tested well above his age level. Today, he's an excellent athlete, a very high achiever, and a chemical engineer in New York City. I wrote about this experience in my books *Maverick Mind* and *The Boy Beyond Reach.*

Because of this personal experience and my years of training, research, and work in this field, I began to develop the concepts and strategies now central to my Brain Engineering programs. I have been able to help enhance the lives and sharpen the skills of thousands of children diagnosed with Autism, ADD, PDD, and other learning disabilities, who are now symptom-free, have strong attention and memory skills, fluent language skills, self-control, and can interact with their families in a stress-free, harmonious way.

AMP Up is an excellent resource for anyone interested in discovering new ideas about how the brain codes and builds knowledge. You will see how children build from attention to memory, to the four processors of listening, reading, speaking, and writing. You will be able to conceptualize how to improve your own brain amplifiers from the illustrations provided.

For some families this manual is enough and the ideas presented will send them on their way with new ideas and insights that they can apply immediately. Other families, however, prefer additional materials and guidance, especially those with children who are having trouble with communication and cognition which result in behavior problems. I have created very specialized materials, including videos, music, and personal consultation, to support your ability, and your child's ability, to learn to "AMP Up."

Please go to www.cheriflorance.com to learn more about how, through Brain Engineering Labs, parents use the book and videos and music CDs, following a step-by-step progression, to help their child learn brain-friendly interactions that are fun and tremendously beneficial. Each family is provided with a private website that houses the videos and songs, a workbook of materials, a performance dashboard, and a puppet theater. Those interested in looking into the complete "AMP Up" program can email me at info@cheriflorance.com.

Dr. Cheri Florance, Ph.D.
Brain Engineering Labs, New York
www.ebrainlabs.com

Dedication and Acknowledgements

I dedicate this book to my beloved mother, Dorothy Fitchhorn Florance. My mother grew up in a family of musicians who loved to play and enjoy music. When she was in college she also played first chair clarinet and harp in the Nashville Symphony. Mother raised my sister Denise and me to love the arts and we were dancing on stage at the age of three and performing in plays at the age of four at the local university.

As a result, I have always used drama, music and dance in my own work as a brain doctor. So the creation of AMP—Attention-Memory-Processing—is a testimony to my mother's inspiration which began when I was a newborn baby.

I would also like to thank the steadfast devotion of my three children who helped me by providing moral support and creativity during the development of this multi-faceted project—Vanessa, a New York City Attorney, and William and Whitney, both Chemical Engineers. Although they are all grown up now and in their own careers, they still find the human brain fascinating and often talk about their own brain engineering around the family table.

Thanks also to my editor Margaret Daisley who worked with me tirelessly, and my current dance and art teachers who stimulate my imagination.

And big hug to all of the parents who helped provide the wonderful illustrations and photographs used in this book. Most of all, thanks to all of the children who loved this project so much and helped to develop a warm fuzzy way to learn.

A very special thanks to our Brain Engineer Dancers and Producer:

Jimmy Allen (dancer) is from Miami, proud to be living in New York City, and comes from a strong background in acting and dance. Jimmy received a B.F.A in acting from Florida International University, and an Acting Certificate from American Conservatory Theater in San Francisco. As a working actor, Jimmy continually stretches himself by studying at The Barrow Group, a recipient of a Drama Desk Award and Obie Award for Off-Off Broadway Excellence.

Tia Zorne (dancer) is thrilled to be a Brain Engineer bringing out her animal side. Since fainting as a Silly Girl in Beauty and the Beast, Tia's other New York credits include ditzy Little Ada in The Cabaret Girl (Musicals Tonight!) as well as the Therapist in She Can't Believe She Said That and was a featured dancer in Freshly Tossed (both NYMF). She's roller-skated in Starlight Express, purred in Cats, and dove from a swinging trapeze as The Princess in an MGM stunt show. Other credits include Choreographer/Artistic Director for Thoroughly Modern Millie (Riverside Dinner Theater).

Marcos Solá (videographer) is also an accomplished singer. *Opera Magazine* described Solá as "an appealing baritone as Belcore" in the 2009 Opera in the Heights production of L'Elisir. His voice has been described as "rich and robust with artistic flair" whether he is singing Mozart or Puccini. With his interest in Spanish music, he was also featured in the two zarzuela video productions by the Jarvis Conservatory, and has recorded La sangre del amor, a recording of songs by Obrados, Roderigo and Turina. More information about Marcos can be found on his website, www.marcos-sola.com.

… the designer of the AMP Up Animals:

Missy Rinaldi is trained in both fine art and digital/graphic arts, and truly loves creating design, but says she works just as much at being a mom to two fabulous, active kids. Ms. Rinaldi recently moved to Virginia, after living in Southern California for 21 years, to be near parents and open a restaurant—which has given her interior sense of design a flex. Three years later, Sirena Cucina Italiana is a fabulous success, thanks to her wonderful husband and a fabulous clientele. She invites you to stop by when you're in Norfolk.

… the singer/songwriter of the AMP Up Animals songs:

Liz Efroymson-Brooks has been writing songs from her Hoosier haven in Indianapolis for over 40 years; her portfolio includes two children's albums and the music for four musicals. She has over 15 years of experience working with children as a preschool music teacher. In her "spare time" she teaches over 30 private cello students and is a freelance cellist. Liz has a B.A in English from Indiana University, a Masters in Secondary Education from Indiana University-Purdue University at Indianapolis, and a Masters in Cello Performance from Butler University. She plays the cello, piano, guitar, and ukulele, and has just started learning to play the tin whistle.

… and the AMP Up editor:

Margaret Daisley has been an editor in New York City since 1996, focusing on non-fiction books, articles, and research reports. She has an M.A. in English from the University of Massachusetts, Amherst and a B.A. in American Studies from Queens College, City University of New York. Nothing pleases her more than helping to nurture a project from inception to publication, especially one as enjoyable and worthwhile as this book and the accompanying song series.

About Dr. Florance

Dr. Cheri Florance pioneered the scientific basis for Brain Engineering. She is a CEO, Brain Scientist, Mother, Doctor, Professor, Author, National Institutes Of Health Researcher, Educational Problem Solver, Corporate Consultant, Board Prep Trainer, International Advisor, Expert Witness, Keynote Speaker, Clinical Director, and hospital-based speech-language pathologist.

Dr. Florance has a dual doctorate in speech/hearing science and psychology from Ohio State University. As a clinical-research fellow for the National Institutes of Health, a premier medical research facility recognized for rigorous excellence world-wide, Dr. Florance examined the neuro-science of human attention-memory and processing for five years. Currently, she develops specialized programs for highly visual thinkers with problems in attention, memory, listening, reading, speaking, and writing. She consults internationally, having recently worked for the Simon and Schuster in London, The Fulbright Commission in Cyprus, The Minister of Education in Greece, and The Department of Education in Moscow, and she was selected by the American-Pakistan Foundation to serve as a U.S. Ambassador on a contingent of noted scientists.

In the United States, Dr. Florance has over 30 years of clinical research and teaching experience, having worked for U.S. governmental agencies, including the U.S. Office of Education, the U.S. Bureau of Education for the Handicapped, and the U.S. Department of Health, Education and Welfare. She was one of the youngest researchers to be named Fellow by The American Speech, Language and Hearing Association, an award given to less than one percent of its members. She has also received the Distinguished Service to Mankind Award from Muskingum College.

Dr. Florance has been interviewed by USA Today, the Today Show, Oprah Winfrey, Hour Magazine, P.M. Magazine, CBS News, and numerous other newspapers and magazines. Her work has been honored by the Mayor of Columbus, Ohio, the Governor of Ohio, and President of the United States. She has been invited to present workshops more than 1,000 times at hospitals, universities, and national meetings, and has set up programs in psychology, speech-language pathology, the neurology of communication, and Maverick Mind training, in school districts internationally. Dr. Florance has served on numerous national panels and committees, and was an editor of The Journal of Speech and Hearing Research. Her office has been selected many times by test developers and corporations as a field site for new tests and equipment.

Table of Contents

Introduction, *14*

- Brain's AMPlifiers = Attention-Memory-Processing
- The Opticoder and the Lexicoder
- The Bi-Modal
- The Maverick Mind
- Refreshing The Brain's AMP

AMPlify Your Brain's Attention: Memory in the USA, *18*

Chapter 1: Activate Visual Attention—*Turtle, 20*

Chapter 2: Activate Auditory Attention—*Caterpillar, 30*

Chapter 3: Visual Memory to Knowledge—*Lizard, 40*

Chapter 4: Lexicoder Memory to Knowledge—*Crocodile, 46*

AMPlify Your Processing Around The World, *54*

Chapter 5: Processing: Listening Input—*Peacock, 56*

Chapter 6: Processing: Speaking Output—*Bear, 76*

Chapter 7: Processing: Reading Input—*Deer, 86*

Chapter 8: Processing: Writing Output—*Stork, 94*

Chapter 9: Brain AMP Cool Down—*Butterfly, 106*

Chapter 10: Brain Circuit Refresher—*Anemone, 114*

Magnificent Maverick Minds Everywhere, *126*

Reading References, *127*

Introduction

Brain's Amplifiers = Attention-Memory-Processing

The Brain is equipped with three systems that can be trained to AMPlify your Brain Engineering. We are all born with our own unique Brain Engineering, our mental template for thinking and communicating. The Amplifiers of this template are Attention-Memory-Processing (AMP). We use our amplifiers to highlight and organize how we code information. We fuel our amplifiers when we sleep at night and then use this brain fuel throughout the day as we think and communicate. The Brain Engineering Amplifiers are

- **A**ttention
- **M**emory
- **P**rocessing

Brain Engineering Amplifiers tend to be inherited or run in families. So if you find a child who appears to be highly visual, there is a good probability that the child's grandparents or parents are highly visual too. About 45% of children are born with Bi-Modal Brain Engineering while 32% are highly visual Opticoders, and 32% are highly verbal Lexicoders. An extreme Opticoder is called a Maverick Mind.

- Bimodal Brain AMP Engineering = 45% of human brains

- Opticoders use visual attention-memory-processing more often = 32%

- Lexicoders who prefer verbal attention-memory-processing = 23%

- Maverick Minds, who have as many as 50 symptoms in attention, memory, listening, reading, speaking and writing because of an over-working visual brain = 15% of the Opticoders

The Opticoder and Lexicoder

We decode information to take information in and store it, and encode information to produce communication. We can do this in two ways: visually—using pictures—or verbally—using words (reading, writing, listening, speaking).

No doubt you have heard people referred to as visual or verbal thinkers. Perhaps you've even tried to classify yourself in one of these two categories and been frustrated because you don't feel that you are just one thing or the other. For instance, if you make your living with words—as a writer, editor, or speaker—you may assume you are a verbal thinker. And yet you also find that you see stories as mini-movies in your mind, or have an affinity for mechanical tasks—all skills that are associated with visual thinkers. The reason it can be confusing is that the way we intuitively define visual and verbal, can be misleading in terms of what brain science tells us about these separate skill areas.

Visual thinking, or **Opticoding**, is one way we can take in information and think. Opticoding is thinking in a non-verbal way, such as taking things apart and putting them together, seeing a mental image of a person while talking on the phone, or jumping to the bottom line by merely skimming the material. When you watch a movie, or imagine a scene in your head, or figure out how to put an IKEA cabinet together by "seeing" the steps (as opposed to reading the instructions) you are using the Opticoder. The Opticoder is a powerful brain system; in fact, it is the dominant brain system among most geniuses, as it is faster, and more efficient. Yet little formal education is offered to the Opticoder. In fact, we can live without an Opticoder.

Verbal thinking, on the other hand, or the **Lexicoder**, is nearly impossible to live without. All formal education relies heavily, if not exclusively, on the Lexicoder: listening, reading, writing, and speaking. Think about it: *all instructions are given with words*. In fact, most brains—about 80% of the population—are organized with the Lexicoder as the primary processor, and the Opticoder as a back-up processor. In other words, most of the population learns using the Lexicoder, and uses the Opticoder for tasks that aren't necessarily formally taught skills. Furthermore, because we are not even aware that we have these distinctly unique operating systems most of us use both Opticoding and Lexicoding at only a tiny percent of these systems' total capacity.

The Opticoder

Every Lexicoder component has a visual analog. In other words, our brains' word processors and video processors are partners. This means that once you have learned something via the Lexicoder, the Opticoder can take that new information or skill and create, analyze, interpret, and comprehend just as effectively as the Lexicoder.

For instance, to learn to do heart surgery, you would have to read books and listen to lectures or instructions. But once you've mastered the skill, you don't need words anymore. You can solve problems that may arise, and do the task using your Opticoder brain. In fact, most surgeons do use their Opticoders for their work.

The Lexicoder

The Lexicoder controls language processing and therefore is essential for learning. Listening and reading are the two ways we input information into our verbal brain; writing and speaking are the two ways we output information from our verbal brain.

The way Lexicoding, or language processing, works is via the brain's auditory processing system. This is another important aspect of understanding the Lexicoder system that often confuses people at first. So let me say it again: *The Lexicoder is fueled by our hearing system.*

Many people ask me, *how can it be that we learn language via our auditory processing system, our hearing system? Aren't reading and writing visual?* When we look at the letters on the page or produce letters when writing, we are using our eyes, this is true. But when we comprehend what we read or generate an idea into writing, most of us need to change the letters to the sound they symbolize.

Consider this example. Write down these words: Cheri, Chair, Cat, and Kitten. Now, circle the letter "C" in each of these words. Read each word to yourself. To do this, you automatically take the visual symbol for "c" and translate it into a sound, what is called a phoneme. For each of these words, the sound of the C or the K is different. You have to know what the letters and words *sound like* to know what the word means. In other words, you have to use your hearing system, in order to understand the meaning of these words. You have to use your auditory processing system to read.

Think about the way we read. When we read we vocalize it into memory. Little kids speak out loud when they are learning to read. They sound out the letters to form words and say the words to form sentences and understand meanings. When we get older we read "silently" to ourselves, but we are still using the auditory processing system. It has just become a faster, seamless process.

When you think about it, most early learning takes place using the Lexicoder system. From birth, we are taught to speak via the auditory processing system, the most complex of all mental tasks. Grown-ups talk to us, repeating words until we learn to speak. Once at school, we learn to read and write. Can you think of anything we learn without using language in some way? We rarely practice being a visual thinker in the first 12 years of life. The Opticoder is not formally groomed.

People with strong Opticoder skills may pick up hobbies like woodshop or art. But visual thinking is not taught systematically. This is why you can survive and even thrive in our world if you have an Opticoder system that is non-existent or under-performing, but you are in serious trouble if your Lexicoder system is not working.

The Bi-Modal

Bi-Modal Brain Engineering means that you can switch back and forth from visual to verbal thinking. Usually verbal is stronger because we have been learning this code day by day and year by year at school. Visual thinking is used to build a bike or decorate a cake—an auxiliary system that can be "switched on" when needed.

The Maverick Mind

A very special group of brains are called Florance Maverick Minds. In a Maverick Mind, the visual brain is very active.

Because of the over-exuberance of the visual brain, the verbal brain can shut down, and not learn its job properly, or it performs inconsistently. As a result, a very specific 50 symptoms emerge, ones which can be easily identified by parents. If a child has visual thinkers in the family tree and at least 25 of the 50 symptoms, then a good prognosis for improvement can be predicted. If a child has over 35 symptoms that match the ideal Maverick Mind, then an excellent prognosis is anticipated.

Note regarding the use of the word "Animals"—Although our title is "AMP Up With The Animals," we use creatures from land, sea, and sky to increase our imagination exuberance.

AMPlify Your Brain's Attention:
Memory in the USA

Maverick Minds are very unique, and yet universal. They are people who are highly visual thinkers who struggle with processing language. Despite symptoms of autism or ADD, Maverick Minds can become, with training, fluent and successful communicators. My AMP Up program has helped Mavericks from every state in the USA, and has been used to train teachers and therapists from east coast to west coast, from north to south. This book presents a mini-circuit for training Maverick Minds to "AMP Up"—to enhance their Attention, Memory, and Processing skills.

This first section covers the four brain pillars that provide a foundation for learning: audio and visual *attention*, and audio and visual *memory*. This is the important First Step in the "Five Steps of Brain Engineering," in which Mavericks learn to use their powerful visual attention and memory systems to form a solid foundation for improving their verbal skills. In this section, Mavericks use their attention and memory to travel in their minds from the Turtle at Turtle Pond by Belvedere Castle in New York City's Central Park, to a California Caterpillar 3,000 miles away, to a Lizard who lives in the Southwestern desert, and then a Crocodile who creeps through the swamps of Florida. In each case, the Animal provides the visual focus for the learning skill. At the same time, Mavericks imitate the movements of each Animal, thereby providing a memory exercise through kinesthetic , or tactile, experience—learning through moving, doing, touching.

Note that CDs and DVDs to accompany this book are available (www.ebrainlabs.com), though this book alone provides a basic guide—a mini-circuit—to the AMP Up learning program. The CD includes music for the Animal lyrics, as well as music for the Magnificent Mavericks song; the DVD shows dancers acting out each Animal's movements to music and lyrics. You can, however, invent your own music or simply chant the song lyrics like a poem, and you can access free Animal videos on the internet. (See especially www.kids.nationalgeographic.com.)

The point of these first exercises is for wonderful Maverick Minds to use their very visual brains to scan, discriminate, and zoom in on various Animals and their activities from place to place, all over the USA. Interacting with the visual experience of the Animals and acting out their movements will help to build the key brain pillars of the AMP Up program—Attention and Memory—as this warm-up song celebrates.

Magnificent Mavericks

Magnificent Mavericks
Definitely the brains to pick
They can see things in their minds
Movies and patterns—it's picture time!
Movies and patterns—it's picture time!

They have rare and wonderful brains
Einstein attention at video games
See a tiny turtle in a great big pond
They look once and they zoom in on. *Zoom—!*

• Chapter 1 •

Activate Visual Attention 3 Ways With The *Turtle*

The Science Of Brain Engineering

Activate Your Opticoder Eyes To Exercise Attention Three Ways

The components of visual attention:

- **The Zoom Lens**

  The visual zoom lens allows the brain to concentrate, focus, and change focus. It helps the brain make sense of what would otherwise be an incoherent jumble of visual input.

  For example, when you look at a picture of a sailboat in the water beneath a sunny sky, you use the zoom lens to distinguish the boat from the water and the sky. Without thinking about it, you can change your focus from the boat to the water, or from the water to the sky.

- **The Discriminator**

  The brain's visual discriminator compares and contrasts what it sees. The discriminator allows the brain to distinguish between objects by identifying characteristics that are similar and characteristics that are different.

  For example, dogs and cats have many traits in common (four legs, two ears, a nose, whiskers) but they are distinguished by a few distinct identifiers (the way they walk, the shape and size of their eyes, nose, and whiskers).

- **The Scanner**

  The visual scanner is the brain's search engine. It allows the brain to scan a set of data quickly to locate key information—for instance, like finding Waldo in a "Where's Waldo" book.

AMP Up With The Animals: Turtle

How This Helps Your Child

By paying attention to each movement of the Turtle as they watch the DVD, children use their Opticoder Eyes. If you stop the video by hitting the pause button, you can ask your child to imitate the movement they see, which helps commit the visual experience to Memory. By breaking the video into parts to imitate, the child is discriminating one movement from another, while also zooming in on the part of the dancer's body that is moving and pushing the curtain behind the dancer into the background. This figure-ground action is called the attention Zoom Lens.

What is it like to be a Turtle? We can see many steps in our Turtle DVD. Children can remember those steps from watching the video and stopping it and acting it out, or by singing the song, or by doing both activities.

The Maverick AMPs Up: Take a look at the photos where Maverick Jack is becoming a Turtle with his mom. After watching the Brain Engineer dancers Tia and Jimmy move along slowly like a Turtle, Jack's mother paused the DVD and Jack imitated what he saw.

Then they watched the Brain Engineers stick their heads back in their shells, so Jack's Mom put a pillow on Jack's back to serve as his shell. All of these activities work to help Jack process the input—first watching and listening, and then moving and imitating the Turtle.

ATTENTION

- **ZOOM IN TO THE WORLD OF THE TURTLE**
- VISUAL - Zoom in on the actions of the Brain Engineer dancers as they imitate the movements of the Timid Turtle. How many actions can you identify?
- AUDITORY - Zoom in on the slow-moving speed of the song and how that teaches you to move like a Turtle.

MEMORY

- **BRAIN ENGINEERING TURTLE MIRROR**
- VISUAL - Remember what a real Turtle is like while you watch and act out the ACTIONS of our Brain Engineers.
- AUDITORY - Remember the real Turtle when you HEAR the melody of the music and sing along.

PROCESSING

- **LIFE LONG VALUE OF VISUAL ATTENTION ZOOM**
- IN-OUT LISTEN-SPEAK - Take photos of your child becoming a Turtle. Put the photos in a deck and have your child pick one, and then act out the movement, the action. Then you pick one and act out the action. Name the action.
- IN-OUT READ-WRITE - Write captions for the pictures and color the Turtle handout. Put the Turtle on a popsicle stick. Play a little bit of the Turtle music and dance with the Turtle puppet.
- Start a "Chapter Book" for saving photos, puppets, and coloring pages.

Lyrics

Timid Little Turtle

Timid Little Turtle, Timid Little Turtle
Timid Little Turtle—"Hi!"
Don't hide away, I'd love to say "hey"
But you're a little too shy

Slowly peak your head out now
Don't give me that old reptile scowl
Flip those flippers off of that log
And try to make friends with that old bull frog

Isn't it fun, isn't it witty?
A turtle living in New York City
A castle with a pond in the Park
He'd a timid little turtle with a great big heart

Create A Chapter Book

Help your child **create a "Chapter Book,"** which will eventually have a chapter for each animal. This will help with the Processing portion of the exercises (Attention, Memory, Processing). These chapters and pages should be kept in a 3-ring binder, so that pages can be added at any time.

Put your child's name on the binder, and create a **Title Page** for each chapter that lists the Animal, the type of setting that the animal lives in (for instance, the Turtle lives in the pond in Central Park), and other features about the animal that your child remembers—how it moves, what it likes to eat, its color, what sounds it makes, if any.

For each animal, a **coloring page** is included at the end of each chapter in this book, as coloring is one of the Processing (output) activities, along with dancing, singing, and writing. Coloring and drawing can be considered forms of "pre-writing."

Pictures can be pasted onto colored paper, if desired.

In the Chapter Book, you can eventually **include all sorts of items:**

- Photos of your child imitating the movements of the animal.
- Photos that your child takes that are associated with the particular animal—for instance, in the Caterpillar chapter, the song mentions leaves and trees. Your child may want to take a photo of a leaf or a tree.
- Photos of friends and relatives imitating the animal.
- Pictures that your child sees in a magazine.
- Pictures and stories that you find together on the Internet.
- Writings and emails to friends and relatives about the animals.

You can also include 3-ring pocket folders to save items that aren't in the usual letter-size shape, such as photos or pictures that haven't yet been pasted into the Chapter Book.

The Maverick AMP Action

Here Jack gets into a turtle mood.
Dr. Florance puts a pillow on him, calling it a shell.

 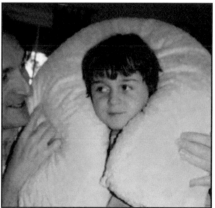

Then he carries the shell on his back for a little while.
When it falls off, Daddy puts it back on.

Then Jack jumps on the bed and asks for his shell, and then hides inside it.

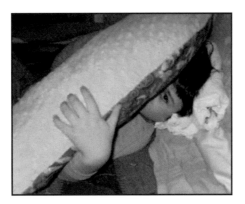 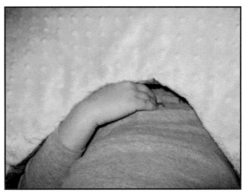

Later when Jack and his sister Maddy watch the Peacock, Jack says "Turtle please. " Jack wants to be the turtle. He is using his Attention Discriminator and his long-term memory.

Turtle please!

Jack peeking out from his shell:

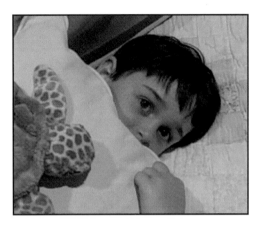

This time Jack invents his own shell and he is processing how to create his own Turtle action. Jack and Mom encourage little sister to become a Turtle too, and now they are in harmony together.

Jack's turtle says, "Shhhhh."   **Maddy's turtle sits in her shell.**

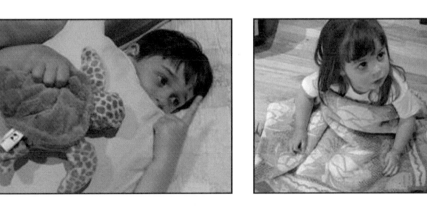

Additional Activities

Go to a website, such as the following, to **watch the turtles**. Type in the word "Turtles" to find a turtle video. Watch the turtles moving slowly. See how the turtle can stick his head down into in his shoulders. See how the turtle moves along slowly and methodically. Keep the real turtle images in mind when imitating the movements of the Turtle Dancers in the video.

- www.video.google.com
- www.kids.nationalgeographic.com

• Chapter 2 •

Activate
Auditory Attention
3 Ways With The *Caterpillar*

The Science Of Brain Engineering

The components of auditory attention:

▪ The Zoom Lens

The auditory zoom lens allows the brain to change hearing focus. You use the auditory zoom lens to sort out the many sounds you hear, so you can use those that are relevant.

For example, if you have ever tried to enjoy a quiet day at the beach, you know what it's like to be virtually assaulted by sound. The waves are crashing, seagulls are calling, radios blare, children laugh and shout, cars in the parking lot start up and brake to a halt. To try to hold a conversation in this setting, or to keep track of your children, you prioritize the sounds that are important.

When you use your auditory zoom lens, you are altering the figure-ground relationship. This means you are pulling information out of the background and bringing it to the foreground.

▪ The Discriminator

The brain's discriminator compares and contrasts what it hears in order to decode incoming words. The discriminator allows the brain to distinguish between sounds. It helps you hear the sounds of words precisely.

Did you hear the word "patch" or "pat"? Did you hear the word "John" or "Sean"? You can also hear a sound like a toilet flushing and identify it. You are discriminating the key sound and determining what it is. The discriminator helps you decipher what you hear and identify it.

▪ The Scanner

The scanner is the brain's search engine. If you are in a restaurant and hear your name at another table, your attention will zoom over to find out what they are talking about. That is your zoom lens in action. But your scanner was already turned on, vigilantly waiting for something important. Your scanner is waiting for your alarm clock to ring to wake you in the morning.

AMP Up With The Animals: Caterpillar

How This Helps Your Child

This time, when your child listens to the song about the Curly Little Caterpillar, have him/her focus on the words of the song on the CD and DVD. See if your child can remember the words and sing along.

When children can do this, they are paying attention to the music in the foreground and the dancers in the background. When they do the movements along with the video they are focusing on the movement more than the singing. That is the difference between auditory and visual attention—they are very different codes.

ATTENTION

- **ZOOM INTO THE WORLD OF THE CATERPILLAR**
  - VISUAL Discriminator - Enjoy the video of the Brain Engineer dancers imitating the movements of Caterpillars. Compare the Caterpillar movements with those of the Turtle.
  - AUDITORY Discriminator - Listen to the song and fill in the missing word.

MEMORY

- **BRAIN ENGINEERING CATERPILLAR MIRROR**
  - VISUAL Discrimination - Look at the pictures of Jacob, Daniel, and Raymond pretending to be Caterpillars. Can you imitate them?
  - AUDITORY Discrmination - Play the CD music for each of the animals, Turtle and Caterpillar, and see if you can sing along with each song.

PROCESSING

- **LIFE LONG VALUE OF AUDITORY ATTENTION DISCRIMINATOR**
  - IN-OUT LISTEN-SPEAK - Building communication partners for conversations: Make copies of the photos of the other children in this book and add to each chapter of the Chapter Book. Share story-telling with your child about each chapter.
  - IN-OUT READ-WRITE - Write captions to the pictures and color the Caterpillar handout. Cut the Caterpillar and Turtle into four parts each (make copies for cutting up). Mix them up and you have a puzzle-processor game.

Curly Little Caterpillar

There are cute little creatures in my own back yard
In the trees, in the garden, I don't have to look hard

Curly Little Caterpillar, rolling in the grass
You have many legs, but you don't move very fast
In a California garden you have quite a paradise
You can build a silky nest and dream of butterflies

You can climb out on a leaf and look down from a tree
Your funny little wiggle is my favorite sight to see
Furry little friend, you like so much to eat
Milkweed and cabbage are your favorite treats

(musical interlude)

Curly Little Caterpillar rolling in the grass
You have many legs, but you don't move very fast
In a California garden you have quite a paradise
You can build a silky nest and dream of butterflies

You can climb out on a leaf and look down from a tree
Your funny little wiggle is my favorite sight to see
Furry little friend, you like so much to eat
But now it's time to say goodbye and softly go to sleep …

Jacob is a Caterpillar

Daniel is a Caterpillar

Raymond is a Caterpillar

 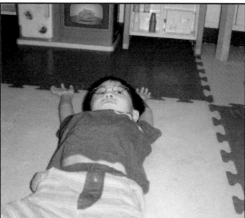

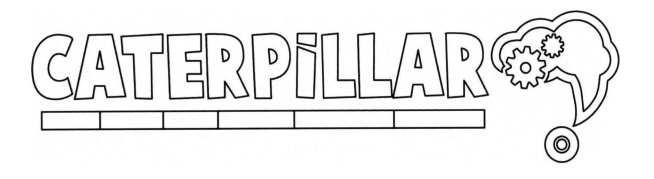

• Chapter 3 •

Move Visual Memory To Knowledge With The *Lizard*

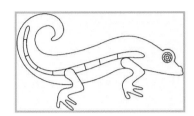

The Science Of Brain Engineering

The Opticoder Engine = Visual Memory

We move input ideas into our brains through our working memory. We have three memory tools that we use to move a thought into knowledge. These tools are:

■ **Bin sorts**

Bin sorting is organizing data into categories, or bins, as the data comes in from immediate memory. There are many ways to sort visual input. The better we are at bin sorting data, the more efficient and flexible we become at thinking, learning, communicating, and relating to others.

■ **Closure**

Closure means completing a thought by filling in the blank or completing the idea. The better we are at closure, the easier it is for us to predict meaning, and that helps us build our bank of ideas. When we close an idea, we connect with a reference point and that allows us to use associations that build patterns of intelligent thinking.

■ **Time**

Time also involves sequencing. Our dancers show you steps in a specific order. The song we hear also has a sequence in time. Sequencing is a very important time-based process that helps us form memories and store and retrieve concepts.

AMP Up With The Animals: Lizard

How This Helps Your Child

When you are learning new ideas, you create a place to store them. You experience exuberance when you learn something brand new. Then you find your reference point and build your filing system around this new idea. When you do this, you move your thoughts from immediate to short-term to long-term memory.

With the Lizard, see if your child can watch the DVD and remember the movements. If so, then the child is using his/her working memory to learn something new. If children can also remember the movements of the Turtle and the Caterpillar in pictures in their minds, they are using their visual long-term memory.

Watch the DVD of the Lizard, pause the DVD after 15 seconds, and have your child repeat the movements. Then watch the DVD again and see how much he/she remembered.

Play the music CD alone and see if your child can do the movements from the Turtle and Caterpillar. If children can remember the movements, they are using their long-term memory.

Next, see if they can identify the actions as they see them while they're watching the animal component before the dancers. Write down each action that your child sees—have the child tell you and you can write them down, or if they are ready, they can write it themselves. Then look at what was written and see if the child can reproduce the movement.

If children can remember and reproduce the movements of the animals from the written form and from long-term memory, then they are using their mirror neurons, which assist them in learning and social skills. So this is a great additional benefit for learning the Lizard.

ATTENTION

- **•ZOOM IN TO THE WORLD OF THE LIZARD**
- •VISUAL - Immediate Memory: Play 10-20 seconds of the DVD and then push the pause button. See if you and your child can imitate what you saw.
- •AUDITORY - Immediate Memory: Play the songs of the three animals and point to the picture in your Chapter Book that goes with the song.

MEMORY

- **•BRAIN ENGINEERING LIZARD MIRROR**
- •VISUAL - Short Term Memory: Make copies of all the pictures of all of the children in this book. Put them in a big pile. Take each coloring page as the base (for example, Lizard). Pick a picture out of the pile and put it on the correct coloring page. Now you are doing a bin-sort.
- •AUDITORY - Short-Term Memory: Play the music CD for each of the three animals. Pause the song and draw a body part of the animal that goes with the song.

PROCESSING

- **•LIFE LONG VALUE OF VISUAL LONG-TERM MEMORY**
- •IN-OUT LISTEN-SPEAK - Make two copies of the pictures. Take 10 pairs and put them face down on the table. Turn them over to make pairs. Put them in the same order 30 minutes later and do it again. See if your child remembers the order from the previous time. Make a master chart of where the pictures are. Give each other hints. Share story-telling with your child about each chapter.
- •IN-OUT READ-WRITE - Take pictures or make copies of all of the animals and all of the children. Then make a collage. See if you can find similarities and differences in colors, shape, and sizes. Write captions for the collages. Save these in the Chapter Book.

Lyrics

Lively Lizard

I see you, Lively Lizard, running through the desert ground
Your dark eyes are regal as you quickly look around
Lively Lizard — fast as a wizard
Scrambling through the sands of New Mexico lands

Look around for a spider or a nice big bug
You can snap it up quickly with your long forked tongue
Your brown and yellow stripes decorate my garden space
Crawling up the wall with quickness and grace

Suddenly there's danger
A wild and wooly stranger

(faster)

Run, my Lizard, run — a coyote's on your trail
Run, my Lizard, run — now he's almost caught your tail
Run, my Lizard, run — in the bright adobe sun
Now you shine in the bright sunlight — boy, you sure have fun

Daniel is a Lizard

Chapter 4

Move Lexicoder Memory To Knowledge With The *Crocodile*

The Science Of Brain Engineering

We are building a circuit that unites attention and memory from both the Opticoder visual pathway and the Lexicoder verbal pathway. That integrated circuit is the biology that supports knowledge management. When we have an idea, we go through a process of spark-fire-fuel-flow to generate a thought. We comprehend what we hear or read or see by interpreting and adding meaning.

On the Opticoder pathway, that process involves forming a thought in the brain's visual-spatial sketchpad using our attention to short-term memory skills. We then interpret the idea by decoding or encoding meaning. Visual people do this by using their brain's Associator. If I tell you that I just returned from watching a movie about a crocodile, then you might see a picture or movie in your visual sketchpad of Crocodile Dundee or the Crocodile and Captain Hook from Peter Pan. You would be making an association with ideas you have stored in your memory to understand my communication. Then you would process the concepts I am sharing and add them to your knowledge files. The Opticoder pathway moves information through the Attention-Sketchpad to the Memory-Associator and the Concept Idea Generator. Then we gear shift the new idea into knowledge using picture files.

The Lexicoder pathway moves an idea from the phono loop—as in *hearing* what you say or *listening* to an internal voice when you read—to the brain's sequencer. The sequencer follows the Agent-Action-Object series to obtain meaning. That means when we process language we need to know the people—the actions and the objects—in order to get the main idea. Agent-action-object comprises 80% of what we hear, say, read or write. The three parts of a sequence give us meaning in phrases and sentences and from them we build paragraph thinking. So, on the Lexicoder pathway we move from Attention-Phono Loop to the Memory-Sequencer to Paragraph Idea Generator, and then we gear shift the idea into knowledge using word files.

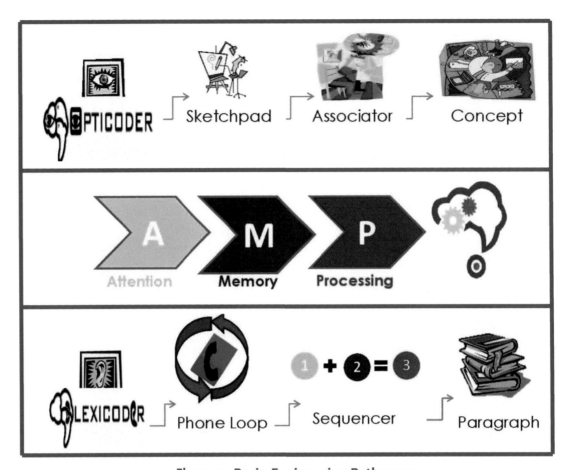

Florance Brain Engineering Pathways

AMP Up With The Animals: Crocodile

How This Helps Your Child

Can your child hum the catchy tunes from the first five songs? Can he/she sing the words? If so—and if they can remember the words—they are using their Lexicoder memory.

If you play the song, and then stop the music, can your child fill in the blank? If so, then they are using closure, which is one of the working memory tools.

Can your child sing the song in time with the music at the speed the singer on the CD is singing it? If so, they are using time, another working memory tool.

If they hear part of the song, can they remember that this song goes with the Crocodile and then hear part of another song and remember that song goes with the Caterpillar or the Turtle? When that happens, they are using working memory bin sort.

ATTENTION

- **ZOOM IN TO THE WORLD OF THE CROCODILE**
- VISUAL - Immediate Memory: Watch and listen to the DVD. Every time you hear the word "Crocodile" point to the Brain Engineers acting like Crocodiles on the computer screen while watching and listening.
- AUDITORY - Immediate Memory: Watch and listen to the DVD. Then sing the song. You sing the word "Creeping" and have your child sing the word "Crocodile," continuing every time to allow your child to fill in the blank.

MEMORY

- **BRAIN ENGINEERING CROCODILE MIRROR**
- VISUAL - Short Term Memory: Put pictures of all four animals in front of your child. Sing a phrase of a song. See if your child can point to the picture of the right animal.
- AUDITORY - Short-Term Memory: Make two Crocodile puppets. Have your child sing in a high voice and a low voice. The high voice says "Creeping." The low voice says "Crocodile." And then you sing the rest of the song lyrics.

PROCESSING

- **LIFE LONG VALUE OF AUDITORY LONG-TERM MEMORY**
- IN-OUT LISTEN-SPEAK - Make agent-action-object cards for each animal. Put these captions under the pictures. For instance: Turtle hides in shell. ("Turtle" = Agent; "hides" = action; "shell" = object). Other examples: Lizard climbs tree. Crocodile snaps his jaws. Listen and speak the message that goes with the pictures.
- IN-OUT READ-WRITE - Mix the words up and put them back in a timeline for the pictures in a comic strip format.

Lyrics

Creeping Crocodile

(Chorus)
Creeping, Creeping Crocodile—How I love his sneaky smile
He's an Amazon reptile—Snap! Snap! Snap!

Crawls so very slowly
Millions of years old, he
Basks in the Brazilian sun, then
Snap, snap, snap! ... It's fun now
Basks in the Brazilian sun, then
Snap, snap, snap! ... You'd better run now

(Chorus)

On the bank he's creeping
Slitty eyes are peeping
Slides into the water and waits ...
Snap! Too late—
Paradise, there's lots of bait ...
Snap! How great!

(Chorus and out)

Keefe is a Crocodile

Raymond is a Crocodile

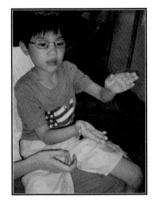  

The Crocodile opens his mouth.

 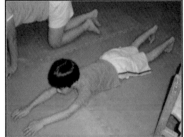 

The Crocodile is crawling.

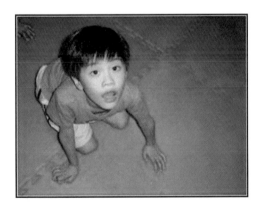 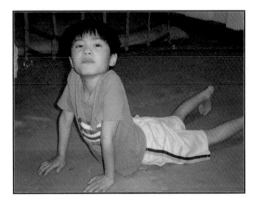

The Crocodile is looking.

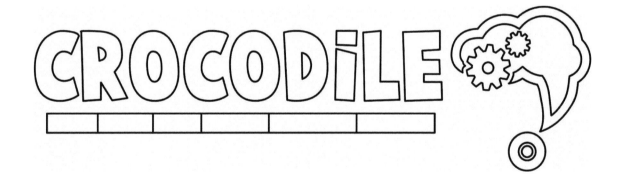

AMPlify Your Processing Around the World

As said previously, Maverick Minds are unique—but they are universal. Highly visual thinkers exist all over the world, and I have worked with families from Bolivia to Greece, Canada to Cyprus, and China to the Philippines. I have consulted with the White House and National Institutes of Health in the USA, the Minister of Education in Greece, the Fulbright Commission in Cyprus, the medical school faculty in Moscow, the BBC in London, and the American-Pakistani Foundation.

Their nationalities may differ, but Maverick Minds share one thing in common—their brains are wired to experience the world first as a visual experience. This sometimes makes them seem like "strangers in a strange land," one where most people experience the world as a verbal, word-based system. And, while most people can live and thrive in the world without a strong visual-based system, living without a verbal system can be devastating. Mavericks are often thought to have autism, ADD—or are even dismissed for "not trying hard enough."

At the same time, their disability is their gift. Mavericks have the advantage of communicating through a mental world of pictures, videos, slide shows, and other visual media. These are people who go on to become architects and artists, engineers and surgeons. This is why I developed the AMP Up program—to help Maverick Minds bridge the gap between their visual and verbal ways of experiencing the world.

In the first section, the focus was on **Step 1** in the **Five Steps of Brain Engineering**: AMPing up audio and visual <u>A</u>ttention, and audio and visual <u>M</u>emory. In the next section, the focus is on the "P" in AMP—<u>P</u>rocessing—and involves the four remaining Steps of Brain Engineering:

- ▪ **Step 2:** Anchoring the Central Executive for self control: Training is aimed at teaching the skills that help build self control of mood, behavior, and communication. The drivers of the Central Executive are the Sequencer and the Associator. What enables a Maverick to become efficient in using language is the ability to channel-switch between the visual and the verbal brain. This helps with skills such as prioritizing, planning, and forecasting thoughts into words.

- ▪ **Step 3:** Developing Input Processors: Training is focused on learning to listen and read, receptive language. This is how human beings move knowledge into the brain. By anchoring the Central Executive, Mavericks are able to use their brain support to control how they manage information. Fluency in thinking and communicating comes from the efficiency in which new ideas move from immediate recall, to short-term memory, to long-term memory. By improving attention and memory, as well as channel-switching, Mavericks are able to move toward a symptom-free life.

■ **Step 4:** Developing Output Processors: Training is focused on learning to speak and write, expressive language. Mavericks use the strength of their receptive language to support speaking and writing. All of our lives we rely on our receptive language to help us encode our ideas from thought to word. We learn through our receptive language, but we are graded by our expressive language. Many of the symptoms of autism or ADD are measured by how someone answers questions or knows how to say the right thing at the right time.

■ **Step 5:** Transferring skills to home, school or work to build self-esteem. This is the ultimate goal of the Five Steps of Brain Engineering and "AMPing Up." Mavericks tend to be highly intuitive and big-picture thinkers. Often Mavericks work from the concept to the details. They associate, rather than working in a linear (verbal) context. Although these phenomenal traits can cause problems initially, when harnessed properly, they propel the Maverick forward, allowing them to use these same skills for processing their verbal experiences.

There are Mavericks all over the world, learning to harness their Central Executive, and process their verbal, as well as their visual worlds. That's the theme of this section, along with a new verse to the "Magnificent Mavericks" song below.

Magnificent Mavericks*

Magnificent Mavericks
Definitely the brains to pick
They can see things in their minds
Movies and patterns—it's picture time!
Movies and patterns—it's picture time!

Coolest Minds in the USA
Geniuses, I'm proud to say
Lizard hiding on a leaf in a tree
Mavericks remember – Mavericks see! *See—!*

*Note that CDs and DVDs to accompany this book are available (www.ebrainlabs.com), though this book alone provides a basic guide to the AMP Up learning program. The CD includes music for the lyrics about each Animal, as well as music for the Magnificent Mavericks song; the DVD shows dancers acting out each Animal's movements to music and lyrics. You can, however, invent your own music or simply chant the song lyrics like a poem, and you can access free Animal videos on the internet. (See especially www.kids.nationalgeographic.com)

• Chapter 5 •

Processing Listening Input With The *Peacock*

The Science Of Brain Engineering

The Brain's Boss is called the Central Executive. The Central Executive controls the AMP Attention-Memory-Processing in terms of prioritizing and planning. We can re-fuel the Central Executive by cardio-exercises, a good night's sleep, or by specially designed exercises. In this DVD we are teaching you how to refresh your own Brain AMP with new fuel from the Central Executive and how to teach your child to do the same.

Throughout childhood, there is a thickening of "gray matter" in the brain. This thickening is caused by an overproduction of connections between brain cells (neurons). This "exuberance," as it is called, seems to be nature's way of ensuring that the brain is prepared to survive and flourish in *any* environment and through *any* circumstance that it encounters. Systematic "pruning" of neural connections means that those that are used remain intact and are strengthened.

Our goal for this DVD is for you to learn how to refuel the Brain's Amp so that you and your child experience the joy and exhilaration of brain exuberance.

Those connections that are *not* used are "pruned," essentially eliminating pathways that *could* have been utilized, but were deemed unnecessary. The phrase "use it, or lose it" is particularly applicable to the Maverick Brain. Utilizing certain neural pathways through life (and school) experiences results in a strengthening of some connections, and an elimination of others. The final product is a brain that is highly efficient and effective— perfectly "sculpted" by its environment and its experiences.

School requires listening 76% of the time, according to The Ohio Department of Education. The most important risk factor for a student is a deficit in listening skills. An estimated 90% of school requirements depend upon successful receptive language.

AMP Up With The Animals: Peacock

How This Helps Your Child

Have your child point to the peacock when he/she hears the word "peacock" in the song. If children can do this, and if they can point to other pictures when they hear the words that identify those pictures, then they are comprehending what they hear.

Precious Peacock

Precious **Peacock** — you're a treasure
Diamond, emerald and ruby feathers

Strutting there by the Banyan tree
Courting pea hens shamelessly

Precious **Peacock** proudly prancing
Jewel of India—your eyes are dancing

Mythical creature—forest bloom
I'm in awe of your beautiful plume

Have your child do the same exercise with the words and pictures on the next page, pointing to the pictures that match the words they hear.

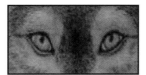

Burning, like she-wolf's eyes,

Burning, like tiger's eyes,

Burning, like fox's eyes,

Burning, like queen's attire,

Shines peacock feathers' fire.

When too tired to hold hide its tail,
The tail folds and disappears.

Breathing deep, its breast spreads like a sail—
Royal screaming everybody hears: "A-A!!"

ATTENTION

- •ZOOM IN TO THE WORLD OF THE PEACOCK
- •VISUALLY - Cued Word Finding: Listen to the beautiful Peacock song. Think about the large swaying feathers of the amazing Peacock. Draw the feathers while you listen.
- •AUDITORY - Take pictures of your child doing the actions of the lyrics and put the pictures above the words to the song. Make a magic wand with Peacock taped to the end of a toothbrush or wooden spoon. Play the song, and when you hear the word that goes with the picture, use the magic wand to point to the picture.

MEMORY

- •BRAIN ENGINEERING PEACOCK MIRROR
- •VISUAL - Cued Key Words: Select three or four key words in the Peacock lyrics for forming associations with the Peacock song. Have your child put these words in order as the song plays. Ask your child what the Brain Engineerdancers do first, then next, and next.
- •AUDITORY - Short-Term Memory: Tell your child a story about the Peacocks that matches the actions in the DVD. Write the story and place the pictures in the sequencing table (see handout). Have your child listen to the story and point to the pictures as you speak.

PROCESSING

- •LIFE LONG VALUE OF LISTENING COMPREHENSION
- •IN-OUT LISTEN-SPEAK - Have your child make up a Peacock sequence story and tell it to you. Make a recording of you and your child telling the Peacock story so you can listen to it later in the car or at lunch or nap time.
- •IN-OUT READ-WRITE - Make sequence stories for all six animals. Make your own podcast or audio tape of the stories so you can listen to them at bedtime. Be sure to save your stories and tape recordings in the Chapter Book.

Lyrics

Precious Peacock

Precious Peacock — you're a treasure
Diamond, emerald and ruby feathers

Strutting there by the Banyan tree
Courting pea hens shamelessly

Precious Peacock proudly prancing
Jewel of India—your eyes are dancing

Mythical creature—forest bloom
I'm in awe of your beautiful plume

Jacob is a Peacock

Sequencing Table

- ■ Tell your child a story about the Peacocks that matches the actions in the DVD. Write the story and place the pictures in the sequencing table. Have your child listen to the story and point to the pictures as you speak.
- ■ Have your child make up a Peacock sequence story and tell it to you. Make a recording of you and your child telling the Peacock story so you can listen to it later in the car or at lunch or nap time.
- ■ Make sequence stories for all six animals. Make your own podcast or audio tape of the stories so you can listen to them at bedtime. Be sure to save your stories and tape recordings in the Chapter Book.

FIRST _____
_____
_____

NEXT _____
_____
_____

THEN _____
_____
_____

FINALLY _____
_____
_____

Agent-Action-Object Exercise

As we build our AMP system, we add a new skill set with each new animal that can then be applied to all of the prior animals. That is how we build our idea generators and our input and output filing and retrieving systems. This exercise focuses on the basic components of a sentence—agent, action, object—which are the basic components of language. To start the exercise, have your child focus on a particular **Action**.

The turtle dancers are sitting down on the floor.

Turtle dancers = **Agents**
Sitting down = **Action**
On the floor = **Object**

John is sitting down **in the high chair.**

Elena is sitting down **taking a picture of herself.**

Luke is sitting down **on a railing.**

Elena and Gia are sitting down **at the picnic table.**

The tiger is sitting down.

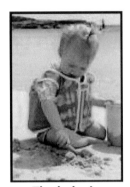

The baby is
sitting down in the sand.

The queen is sitting down
on her throne.

The elephant is sitting down taking a bath.

The horse is sitting down.

Seth, Mindi, and their dog
are sitting down doing refreshers.

Seth is sitting down
eating the food in sequence.

Caterpillar Action Word: Moving

The dancers are moving like a caterpillar.

Elena is moving like a caterpillar.

The Caterpillar puppet is moving on the floor.

Raymond Caterpillar is moving.

Jacob Caterpillar is moving.

The two men are moving the couch.

The cars are moving fast.

This is a moving truck.

The elephants are moving.

These are moving arrows.

The bubbles are moving.

Moving pictures.

Action Word for Lizard: See

The lizard can see.

The lizard dancers can see other lizards.

Everyone can see Elena's water balloon.

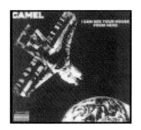

The astronaut can see earth.

The lady can see clearly through her glasses.

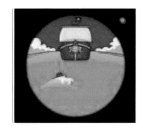

The person can see through the telescope.

I can see clouds through the window.

She can see the view through the binoculars.

Peacock Story
By Elena Proctor

Action Word: *Glow*

The peacock opens his wings. He blows up and lets the feathers sit.

Action word: The peacock glows.

The peacock dancers glow.

Elena Peacock is glowing.

The peacock puppet is letting himself glow.

What else will glow?

The sneaker can glow in the dark.

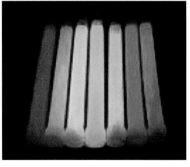

The glow stick rainbow can glow at night.

The stars glow.

Elena ballerina gives a glowing show.

The rainbow and the lightning glow.

The lightning bugs glow in the jar.

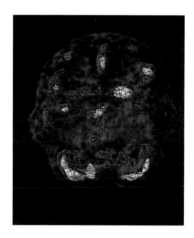

The brain scan glows.

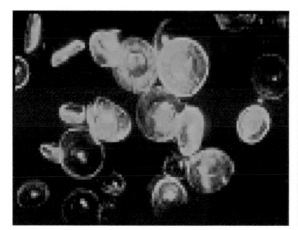

The jellyfish glow.

The cat's eyes glow in the dark.

• Chapter 6 •

Processing Speaking Output With The *Bear*

The Science Of Brain Engineering

Approximately 90% of schoolwork depends upon successful receptive language. Ten percent of schoolwork depends upon expressive language.

That 10% expressive language output is critically important because it is what determines success or failure in school. Output is what is evaluated to determine a student's academic competence. Evaluation of the spoken word by others also determines the student's social acceptance.

AMP Up With The Animals: Bear

How This Helps Your Child

To increase expressive language processing and the act of speaking, we need to develop a reference point. Go to www.kids.nationalgeographic.com and type in the word "bear" to find videos of various bears. By first watching real bears, and then watching the Brain Engineer dancers, we develop two very different reference points. One is concrete—the real bears moving, playing, standing. Then the abstract, the Brain Engineers pretending to be bears. When we talk, we move back and forth from concrete to abstract.

Here are some exercises you can do with your child:

1.   If you go to Google (www.google.com) and type in the word "Bear," you see lots of pictures of bears:

2. Now, type in the word "is" in Google. What do you see? It's not quite as easy to picture the word "is."

3. Now, type in the word "Standing" and you will see images such as this:

Language for the picture thinker can be as confusing as typing these words into Google and coming up with the various images. When visual people hear language they most often store the ideas in a mental file by associating with a reference point. When we speak, we go to that mental file to find the word and then express our ideas by stringing the words together in a motor sequence.

You can see how hard it can be to move from pictures to words by the images we download for the word string BEAR IS STANDING. Eighty percent of what adults say is based on word strings like this, an Agent-Action-Object string. In this instance, Bear is the AGENT. Watch the bear video clips with your child. Identify the ACTIONS that you see the Bears doing. In the song about the Bellowing Bear, "berries" is the OBJECT):

1. WALKING
2. STANDING
3. PLAYING
4. PICKING BERRIES
5. EATING BERRIES

Then take pictures of your child becoming the Bellowing Bear and write captions for each picture. Teach your child how to look at the pictures and tell you the story.

Have your child try to teach the Bellowing Bear song to someone else. The object here is to learn it, remember it, and then teach it. After that, have them try to teach the earlier songs to a playmate or relative.

ATTENTION

- •ZOOM IN TO THE WORLD OF THE BEAR
- •VISUALLY - Cued Speech: Use the Brain Sandwich handout to organize your thoughts about the Bear. Think about the Top Bun, Tomato, Lettuce, Bottom Bun as a paragraph of speech. Color each part of the Brain Sandwich lightly.
- •AUDITORY - Watch the video and listen to the song CD. Pay attention to what happens first, then next, then next. Then stop the DVD and talk about it, imitate it, and take photos.

MEMORY

- •BRAIN ENGINEERING BEAR MIRROR
- •VISUAL - Cued Key Words: Have your child put the pictures in order to make a comic strip.
- •AUDITORY - Short-Term Memory: Write down what your child tells you are the captions to each picture.

PROCESSING

- •LIFE LONG VALUE OF SPEAKING FLUENCY
- •IN-OUT LISTEN-SPEAK - Discuss your topic sentence and three details in consultation with your child.
- •IN-OUT READ-WRITE - Put your ideas into the Brain Sandwich in pictures and words. Put your sandwich into the Basket for Animals (see handout). Make another basket for Water Creatures and another basket for Flying Creatures. Make Brain Sandwiches for them also.

Lyrics

Bellowing Bear

It's lots and lots of fun to watch the Bellowing Bear
Roaring out as if to talk, picking berries everywhere

He grabs so many berries he can hardly hold them all
Then he drops them —GRRR—it's quite comical

Stomping through the English countryside like some great lord
Picking all the berries he can find and then wants more

Stomp! Stomp! Stomp! Stomp! Roar!

Lily watches the Bear DVD.

She lifts her paw.

The Bear has a paw with claws.

Lily Bear eats the berries.

Elena studies the Brain Engineers imitating Bears.

Elena watches the dancers and growls like a Bear.

She pretends to be a Bear picking up pine cones and berries.

Five-year-old Elena takes a picture of a pine cone with her new camera.

Brain Sandwich Chart

Use the Brain Sandwich to organize your thoughts about Bear. Think about the Top Bun, Tomato, Lettuce, Bottom Bun as a paragraph of speech. Color each part of the Brain Sandwich lightly. For example:

Brain Sandwich Topic: Bear Plays and Find Berries

Details:
- Bear plays and stomps through the woods.
- Bear discovers berries and thinks they will be good to eat.
- Bear has too many berries and drops some of them.

Conclusion: Bear is angry and roars!

Topic:

Detail:

Detail:

Detail:

Concluding Sentence:

Baskets For Animals

- Put your Bear Brain Sandwich in the Basket for Animals.
- Make another basket for Water Creatures and another basket for Flying Creatures.
- Make Brain Sandwiches for the other creatures also.

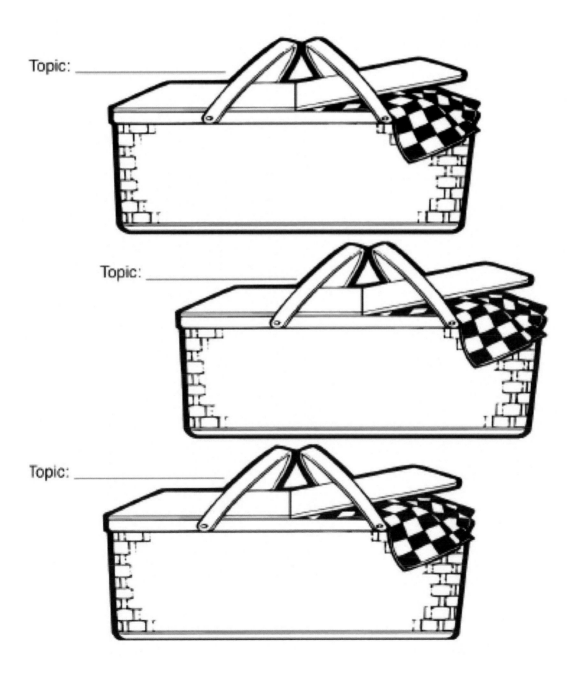

Topic: _____

Topic: _____

Topic: _____

• Chapter 7 •

Processing Reading Input With The *Deer*

The Science Of Brain Engineering

Reading is a code (Lexi-CODER) that is used in conjunction with listening. We listen to a lecture and add to the incoming ideas from reading the assignment.

Reading is one method we use to gain knowledge and ideas from others. We are able to learn, understand and comprehend through reading. From reading we create knowledge files of information and the more organized these files are, the more we can then build our own unique creative output.

About 80% of school depends on the accurate mastery of receptive language processors. Listening and reading become the tools to success. However, how we file that knowledge is critically important because we will be tested on what we REMEMBER. And that is where our grade comes from so we can pass the class and advance.

What is hard for visual thinkers and reading is that reading is a very passive process and visual brains are fast and interactive. To make reading go from the printed page to working memory and then to knowledge we need to make reading an interactive process.

AMP Up With The Animals: Deer

How This Helps Your Child

By now, you should have a growing Chapter Book. As with previous exercises, you can take pictures of you and your child, and possibly other children or significant others, re-enacting all of the animals we have done so far. Write a story using Agent-Action-Object for each animal and take pictures to go with the story. Use the song lyrics to highlight the action and the forward-moving flow of ideas.

The focus in this chapter is reading as input, so be sure to read the Chapter Book to your child. If he/she loses attention while you are reading, have your child match a picture to the picture in the book or a part of a picture to the page in the book. After you read two pages go back and re-read, but this time leave blanks in your oral reading for the child to fill in.

To go along with this reading activity, you can create big, bold sentence captions for the pictures using a computer. For instance, in Microsoft Word use Arial Black font and Bold 20-point font. Cut the sentence strings into single words – such as:

DEER   IS   STANDING

See if your child can put the words in order to tell the story. If this is too hard, just use the key words—the Agent and the Action words—for instance:

DEER   STANDING
DEER   EATING
DEER   WALKING

ATTENTION

- •**ZOOM IN TO THE WORLD OF THE DEER**
- •VISUALLY - Examine the movements of the real Deer (on www.kids.nationalgeographic.com) and then of Brain Engineer dancers. What are the moves of the head and those of the body?
- •AUDITORY - Listen to the varying rhythms of the music and note the varying speeds of the Deer.

MEMORY

- •**BRAIN ENGINEERING DEER MIRROR**
- •VISUAL - Remember the slow Deer and enact those movements. Remember the running, dancing Deer and enact those movements. Be the front of the Deer and then change and be the body.
- •AUDITORY Short-Term Memory - Create two Deer characters , give them names and favorite foods, TV shows, drinks, pet peeves, and settings, using the partnership form (see handout).

PROCESSING

- •**LIFE LONG VALUE OF READING TO COMMUNICATE**
- •IN-OUT LISTEN-SPEAK - Discuss your characters and create a joint story with beginning, middle, and end.
- •IN-OUT READ-WRITE - Write one idea on your own Partnership Form, then pass it to your child. Write the next idea on your child's form. Your child reads what you wrote, and adds in the next block and passes it back and so forth.

Lyrics

Dashing Deer

(Slow – and then fast "Can Can" music)

Dashing Deer, you grew up in the wild
In a "Magnifique" forest, a sweet and gentle child
Now your legs have grown long, your antlers big and strong
You're the finest deer in France—let's do a little dance

Dashing Deer, you're so much fun
You like to kick your heels and run
You're a big red strapping stag
Your little tail is quick to wag

If you think the fruit looks great
You stop awhile to ruminate
Off again, so cavalier
Life is good for Dashing Deer

So be merry—take it in and celebrate
But be wary—sometimes hunters lie in wait
Leaves and pine cones—all the pleasures of the woods
Take it all in—Dashing Deer, your life is good

Daniel
is a Deer

Raymond is a Deer

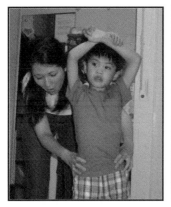

Reading-To-Communication Partnerships

■ Create two Deer characters, give them names and favorite foods, TV shows, drinks, pet peeves, and settings, using the partnership forms below, one for you and one for your child.

■ Write one idea on your own form, then pass it to your child. Write the next idea on your child's form. Your child reads what you wrote, and adds something new in the next block. Continue passing these back and forth, adding to each others' forms.

PARTNERSHIP FORM

TITLE: _____

AUTHOR: _____

ILLUSTRATOR: _____

CHARACTERS:	SETTING:

1.	2.	3.
4.	5.	6.

• Chapter 8 •

Processing Writing Output With The *Stork*

The Science Of Brain Engineering

Writing is a code (Lexi-CODER) that we use to express our ideas or answer questions. It's a durable, portable way to convey our own ideas and to experience the ideas of others. A written language exists in conjunction with a spoken or gestural language. No natural languages exist purely in written form.

Writing is one method we use to express ourselves with language. Expressive language allows us to share our minds, hearts, and souls with others. It demonstrates that we are unique individuals, with our own thoughts and ideas. There are many different forms of expressive language, including discussion, debating, summarization, exhorting, comparing and contrasting, persuasion, investigation, negotiation, instruction, and story-telling.

AMP Up With The Animals: Stork

How This Helps Your Child
Increase your Chapter Book to Chapter 8 and send the chapters by email to a relative or friend. Maybe Grandma, for example, would like to see how your child is able to act like these nine animals. Have Grandma—or another relative or friend—write back one question about each chapter for you to answer.

Write your answers with your child and send them back. Have Grandma, or another relative or friend, find facts about each animal such as its habitat or food preferences and send them to you to add to your book. Include these in your chapters. (The National Geographic for Kids website is a great place to get lots of facts about the animals: www.kids.nationalgeographic.com.)

Now you are using both reading and writing as a very interactive pen-pal method of communicating.

ATTENTION

- •**ZOOM IN TO THE WORLD OF THE STORK**
- •VISUALLY - Find a video of Storks on the internet. Zoom in on three ideas about the Storks that you like while watching the real Storks move.
- •AUDITORY - Put the ideas into words and write them on your Verbal Bin Sort worksheet (see handout).

MEMORY

- •**BRAIN ENGINEERING STORK MIRROR**
- •VISUAL - Watch the Brain Engineers dance, and identify three ideas about each of the Brain Engineers dancers that you like. Put those on Verbal Bin Sort worksheets.
- •AUDITORY Short-Term Memory - Put your ideas to work on the Verbal Bin Sort worksheets.

PROCESSING

- •**LIFE LONG VALUE OF WRITING FLUENCY**
- •IN-OUT LISTEN-SPEAK - Discuss Verbal Bin Sorts for all eight animals.
- •IN-OUT READ-WRITE - Put your ideas on one Maxi for your favorite three animals (see handout), and put your child's favorite three animals on another Maxi for reading and writing.

Lyrics

Soaring Stork

Soaring Stork—you're gliding so high
Storks are writing pretty poems and stories in the Asian sky
Long legs stretching out through the clouds
Silently, solemnly without a sound

Round and round you circle over the tall trees
All over China—the wonders that you see
Deserts and mountains, the Great Wall is the best
When you get tired, you'll go home to your nest

Raymond is a Stork

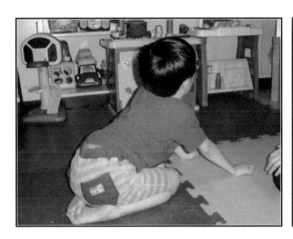

Verbal Bin Sorts

- Zoom in on three ideas about the Stork that you like while watching the real birds.
- Put the ideas into words and write them on your Bin Sorts in the "fact/example" boxes.

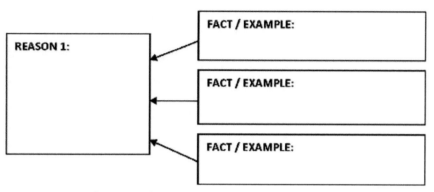

- Watch the Brain Engineers dance, and identify three ideas about each of the Brain Engineers dancers that you like. Put those on Bin Sorts. Figure out the reason why you like these ideas.

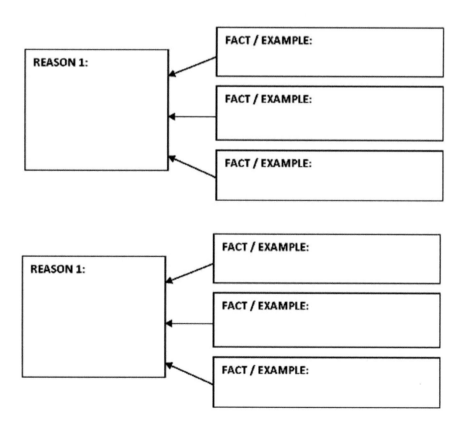

- Do Verbal Bin Sorts for all eight animals.
- Put your ideas on one Maxi for your favorite three animals, and put your child's favorite three animals on another Maxi.
- The three favorite animals can be listed in the "Reason" box.
- The goal is to try to find a conclusion, like you did with the Brain Sandwich.

Verbal Bin Sort
Maxi

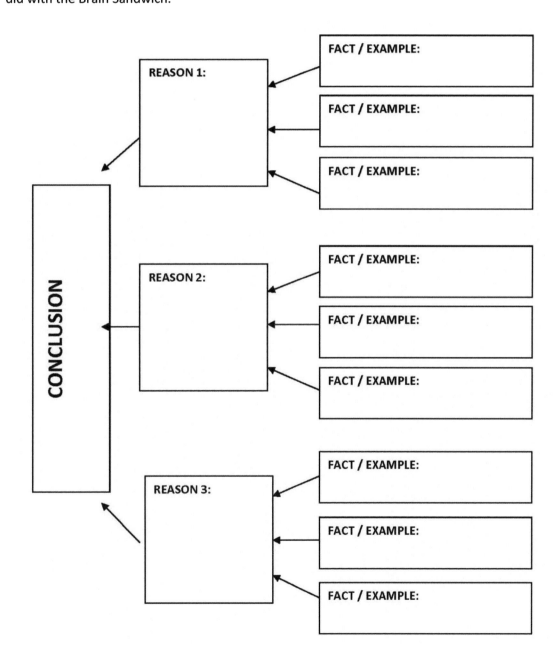

Writing ... And More

We use writing and drawing to tie all of the ideas together that we have learned by AMPing with the Animals. Now we can complete the chapters with photos, drawings, text for reading, and original stories. To stretch the writing process we can use Brain Minis, Brain Maxis, and Cause and Effect.

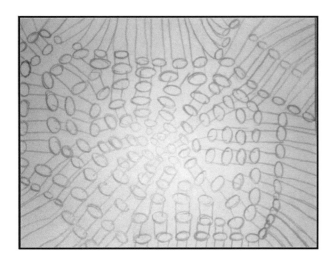

Drawing and coloring are forms of pre-writing. Draw your own illustrations of the animals, like Olivia drew of this Sea Anemone (from Chapter 10). Include the illustrations in your Chapter Book. Work on these activities together with your child. If drawing is too hard for your child to do independently, then use a dot-to-dot method of creating your picture and take turns connecting the dots.

Writing Lessons For The Chapter Book

For the Chapter Book, include an animal Brain Sandwich for each chapter like the one you did for Bear (see handout in Chapter 6, page 81). For instance:

Brain Sandwich Topic: Creeping Crocodile

Details:
- Crocodile sleeps in the sun
- Crocodile swims in the water
- When crocodile snaps, it's funny and exciting

Conclusion: The creeping crocodile makes me laugh when he snaps!

Cause And Effect

Use the "Cause and Effect" chart below to create stories that explain WHY something happens to each of the animals. For instance:

1. Why does the Turtle tuck his head into his shell? (Effect) Because he's shy. (Cause)

2. Why does the Lizard look from side to side? (Effect) Because it scans for danger. (Cause)

3. Why does the bear pick berries? (Effect) Because he thinks they will be good to eat. (Cause)

4. Why does the bear get angry? (Effect) Because he has so many berries that he drops some of them. (Cause)

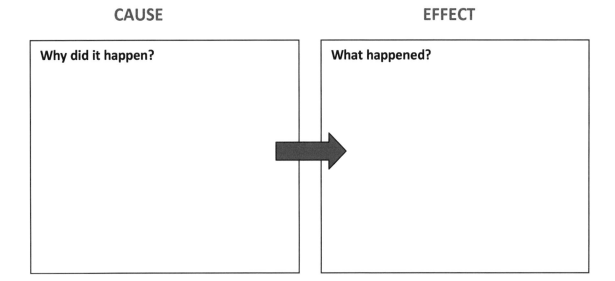

CAUSE	EFFECT
Why did it happen?	**What happened?**

Stork Story
By
Elena Procter

The stork is flying in the air … the air … the air …

It goes so high, it circles over the tall trees.
I want to fly like the Stork.

I'm like the Stork—flying so high, high, high …

When I get tired, I go home to my nest. The End.

STORK

• Chapter 9 •

Brain AMP Cool Down
With The *Butterfly*

The Science Of Brain Engineering

Benefits of AMPing Up Your Opticoder

While you may be able to get through life without a highly developed Opticoder, there are many benefits to building this brain system that will help you thrive. Developing your Opticoder can help you:

- Get to the bottom line quicker
- See solutions to big picture problems faster
- Pick up cues from people's body language and affect, giving you a competitive edge in building relations and negotiating business deals
- Create multiple solutions to problems
- Increase your creativity and sixth sense intuition
- Be first with the right answer
- Improve your ability to build, make, and invent things
- Develop outside-the-box thinking
- Create novel presentations of ideas
- Enhance ways of teaching others, presenting business goals

Benefits of AMPing Up Your Lexicoder

Most of the Mavericks I work with in my practice (strong Opticoders and weak Lexicoders) are successful business executives, but report communication problems that have a crippling impact on their personal lives. They don't know how to communicate interpersonally; they have often tuned out their spouses. Becoming better Lexicoders increases the richness of human relationships. It can also help you:

- Read better
- Remember more
- Remember people's names
- Learn better in academic situations and meetings
- Make more money and get promotions because you're more accurate and efficient
- Have better intimate relationships and a better love life
- Increase your ability to connect with people
- Become a better communicator
- Improve your grades
- Be able to see multiple solutions to problems

Benefits of AMPing Up a Bi-Modal Brain

Once you've built your Lexicoder and Opticoder into superior systems, you can combine them to be able to use your verbal and visual systems simultaneously. Like people who are bilingual, translators can think in two languages at a time. You can build a Bi-Modal Brain to use verbal visual thinking at the same time.

The benefits of building a Bi-Modal Brain include:

- Create better solutions to problems
- Have access to multiple ways to explain your ideas, making your communication more effective
- Be able to convert from one kind of thought to another so you can translate between verbal and visual thinkers
- Be a better manager
- Become a whiz at matching the right person to the right job

AMP Up With The Animals: Butterfly

How This Helps Your Child

We have AMPed up your child's attention, memory, listening, speaking, reading and writing. Now it is time to AMP down with the beautiful Butterfly and relax your child's AMP for re-fueling.

Have your child watch the Butterfly DVD and listen to our Butterfly song. Relax like our Brain Engineers do. See how they calm down after a busy dance to the sleeping pose.

The Butterfly is a beautiful creature. The Brain Engineers have created lovely cool down movements which end in falling asleep. Use this exercise to complete your circuit training.

Now that you have done nine animals, you can replay the DVDs and dance to them all. Warm up with Maverick Music, AMP up with all of the variety of movements and ideas as you go through the wonderful variety of creatures. And then cool down with the Butterfly for a wonderful, relaxing way to end the series of brain exercises.

- **ZOOM IN TO THE WORLD OF THE BUTTERFLY**
- VISUALLY - Watch the beautiful Butterflies and absorb the whole concept.
- AUDITORY - Enjoy the beautiful Butterfly song as you cool down your brain.

- **BRAIN ENGINEERING BEAR MIRROR**
- VISUAL - After watching the video, close your eyes and see if you can imagine the Butterflies.
- AUDITORY Short-Term Memory: Hum along with the music as you relax and refresh.

- **LIFE LONG VALUE OF SPEAKING FLUENCY**
- IN-OUT LISTEN-SPEAK - After the DVD is over, see if you can hear the music in your head.
- IN-OUT READ-WRITE - Allow your mind, and encourage your child, to drift to other thoughts and ideas for a few minutes and then each of you write down your mind's wanderings. Read what your communication partner has written.

Beautiful Butterfly

La la la la la la la la la la la la la la la ...

Beautiful Butterfly, you can fly so gracefully
In the tropical forest, it's magical
Rainbow colors, so happy
You flit from flower to flower
And taste the nectar so sweet
It makes you dizzy and you keep turn, turn, turning all around

You're so delicate and fragile
I want to keep you safe from harm
The Costa Rican woods surround you
Keep you safe in its green arms

La la la la la la la la la la la la la la la ...

Elena is a Butterfly

Daniel is a Butterfly

 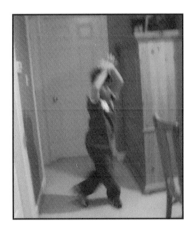 

BUTTERFLY

• Chapter 10 •

Brain Circuit Refresher With The *Sea Anemone*

The Science Of Brain Engineering

How Important Is The *Opticoder*?

Approximately 32% of the population is born with a visual brain—the Opticoder system is their first language. This means that these people prefer to use their Opticoder to think and process information, just as a small percentage of the population prefers to use their left hand. At birth, these babies decode the world around them through visual analogies rather than verbal reasoning. They store knowledge in mental slide trays and movie reels. Often speech, reading, spelling and writing can seem cumbersome and slow.

Careers such as surgery, electrical engineering, computer science, printing, and art depend heavily on the Opticoder. However, without word-based knowledge, none of these skills can be acquired, nor can they advance to the next level.

If you are a surgeon, you must still talk to patients, write chart notes, read medical journals, attend committee meetings, and exchange information with colleagues. There is no escaping the Lexicoder's importance in daily life. It is relatively easy to develop a productive life that contains very little need for the Opticoder. We can shut our eyes and give the Opticoder a rest. We may use our Opticoder much more sparingly. Driving the car, playing tennis, designing a flower arrangement, conceptualizing a flow chart, orchestrating a piece of music, performing a heart operation—all involve the use of the Opticoder.

Still, though Lexicoder communication skills are what distinguish humans from all other species, the Opticoders throughout history are the most famous, make the most money, and tend to leave the most lasting legacies. Opticoding is faster, outside-the-box thinking that has resulted in some of the world's greatest inventions and creative contributions.

How Important Is the *Lexicoder*?

Human communication is essential for life. When Helen Keller was asked if she thought it was worse to be blind or deaf, she said neither. "The handicap I find the worst is my inability to communicate like others because it isolates me from the rest of my species." Helen was a superior reader and writer but that was not enough to give her what she perceived as a quality life.

The Lexicoder is needed for learning, loving, and achieving. To get thoughts into and out of the brain, people use words. Verbal communication accounts for:

- 76 % of learning in the classroom,
- 85 % of career activity,
- 90 % of love affair intimacy and long-term bonding,
- 95% of parent-child shepherding and guidance.

Most humans rely on the Lexicoder 24 hours a day, 7 days a week. We cannot shut our ears. We awaken to an alarm clock, pull the car over when we hear a siren, and answer a ringing phone—which means our hearing vigilance is always on duty. So in addition to the Lexicoder serving as the genetic basis for communication, learning, and relating, we practice using the Lexicoder nearly all of the time.

Further, our educational system devotes the majority of time training us to improve spelling, writing, speaking in front of the group, and comprehending reading passages—all of which require us to practice using our Lexicoders in a step-by-step, sequential building pattern to improve efficiency. The first grader is reading and listening to much less sophisticated language than the 9th grader; a college freshman class is much less demanding in terms of language processing than a medical school lecture. We are training and building our Lexicoder throughout our lives.

AMP Up With The Animals: Sea Anemone

How This Helps Your Child

The Brain AMP (attention-memory-processing) is like a highlighter pen. It is as if we are taking a highlighter into your brain and marking the systems we want to activate. Our goal is to first AMPlify the visual brain—the Opticoder—so we can use that strength to AMPlify the Lexicoder.

When children imitate the patterns they see when watching the video, they are using their Opticoder. When they listen to songs about the Animals, they are using their Lexicoder. When they imitate the movements of the dancers on the DVDs, they are associating what they are doing with what our Brain Engineers are showing them. They are processing concepts.

If they remember this later and can do it with the music only, they are using their long-term Opticoder memory. So then they have AMPed up—activated attention, memory, and processing. See if your child can sing the song the next day after watching the DVD and listening to the music CD. When they can do that, they have moved this knowledge from attention to memory on the Lexicoder pathway.

When your child listens to the music, try to pull out key words. Play the song, and then stop the music and fill in the blank. You can say or sing the word "Awesome"—and see if the child can fill in the next word, "Anemone." When they do this, they are using their "Zoom Lens" to fill in the blank, and using closure from working memory to help find the word.

If children can sing the song along with the movements, then they are using their Bi-Modal Brain Engineering. They are using both systems together.

ATTENTION

- •ZOOM IN TO THE WORLD OF THE SEA ANEMONE
- •VISUAL - Look at the Brain Engineers acting like Sea Anemones on the DVD.
- •AUDITORY - Listen to the Awesome Anemone song on the CD.

MEMORY

- •BRAIN ENGINEERING SEA AMENONE MIRROR
- •VISUAL - Remember the Awesome Anemone while you watch and act out the movements of our Brain Engineer dancers. Move your arms and feet like Tia does. Sway back and forth like Jimmy.
- •AUDITORY - Remember the Awesome Anemone and you hear the swaying melody of the music and hum along or sing along.

PROCESSING

- •LIFE LONG VALUE
- •IN-OUT LISTEN-SPEAK - Take photos of your child becoming an Awesome Anemone. Discuss the movements the child makes to imitate the Anemone.
- •IN-OUT READ-WRITE - Write captions to the pictures and color the Anemone handout. Put the Anemone on a popcycle stick so you can sway with the puppet. Put them in the Chapter Book to save the coloring pages, photos, and other mementos of output activities associated with each animal.

Lyrics

Awesome Anemone

Awesome, Awesome Anemone
You're a strange and wonderful mystery
So many shapes and colors—so bright
Flowery fingers reaching for light

An island blossom, strange and awesome
Anemone, Anemone

Your friend, the clownfish is always near
The Philippine sun shines fine and clear

In your busy coral home, you're never alone
Anemone, Anemone

Awesome, Awesome Anemone
You're a strange and wonderful mystery
So many shapes and colors – so bright
Flowery fingers reaching for light

Anemone, Anemone

Olivia becomes a Sea Anemone while she watches Brain Engineers Tia and Jimmy.

A Happy Brain!

Agent-Action–Object Exercise

As your child continues to invent mini-stories about the Anemone and the other Animals, they are reviewing the Agent-Action-Object exercise and working on their expressive language skills. As before, start with a focus on the Action. The Agent of that Action will naturally follow.

The Sea Anemone is grabbing the light.

Sea Anemone = Agent
Grabbing = Action
Light = Object

Sea Anemone grabbing

Grabbing

Grabbing

Jocelyn and Jack grabbing.

Elena grabbing.

Grabbing hands.

Grabbing hair.

Grabbing a sandwich.

Candy machine grabbing claw.

Bear grabbing the tree.

Baby grabbing the ball.

Leah is grabbing the stuffed animal. She and Gia are having a "clean up the tent" contest.

Gia is grabbing glass pieces for stone step craft.

Luke is grabbing a pencil.

Charlie is grabbing a soda.

Johnny is grabbing a cup of juice.

Writing About The Animals

Now that we have done all 10 animals, think about which three you like the most. Work with your child to decide which ones are your favorites and which are your child's favorites, and even which ones are each family member's favorites.

List at least three reasons why these are the favorites, and then compare and contrast the differences and similarities in each person's favorites. Take all of this information and send an email to Grandma and Grandpa or other significant loved ones and see if they agree or disagree. Now you are writing to communicate!

Before deciding on the three favorite animals, first take six baskets (see Chapter 6, page 82 for the Baskets handout) and think of any ideas about six different animals. For instance:

■ The Awesome Anemone is relaxed on the ocean floor.
■ The Deer clip clops around, and we get to take turns being the head and body.

Sort the ideas into picnic baskets, and then look over all six baskets and divide into "favorite" and "not favorite" until you have your top three.

As always, save these writings in the Chapter Book for reading enjoyment later.

Magnificent Maverick Minds Everywhere

The Maverick Mind is a universal phenomena, not restricted to a particular place, or even a particular time—Einstein, Edison, and Da Vinci have all been labeled highly visual thinkers, though there was no such concept of being a "visual thinker" during their lifetimes. As mentioned in my note to readers early in this book, working with visual thinkers was already my life's work when my third child, Whitney, came into my life and was diagnosed as autistic. Since that time, working with Mavericks has become my life's passion. The AMP Up program developed out of these experiences.

On my website (www.ebrainlabs.com), you can watch the video, *Understanding the Maverick Mind*, which describes Whitney's experience, as well as the experiences of other Maverick Minds who have "re-engineered" their brains, and who are now symptom-free. You can also watch my video *The Five Steps of Brain Engineering* for more information about how "AMPing UP" works.

If you have a child who is suffering from communication problems, or feel you might be a Maverick whose visual-based brain may be hampering your work or personal relationships, the next step is to have an evaluation, which can be done "live" in my virtual online classroom. To find out more about scheduling, go to www.ebrainlabs.com or send me a personal note at: info@cheriflorance.com.

In the meantime, I am hoping people around the world will use this book to AMP Up—train and enhance their attention, memory, and processing skills. To celebrate Magnificent Mavericks everywhere, here is an additional verse to the Magnificent Mavericks song:

Magnificent Mavericks*

Magnificent Mavericks
Definitely the brains to pick
They can see things in their minds
Movies and patterns—it's picture time!
Movies and patterns—it's picture time!

Mavericks process—lightening speed!
Puzzles and legos—they take the lead
Peacocks , storks ,and butterflies
Mavericks imagine they can fly! *Fly!*

*Note that CDs and DVDs to accompany this book are available (www.ebrainlabs.com), though this book alone provides a basic guide to the AMP Up learning program. The CD includes music for the lyrics about each Animal, as well as music for the Magnificent Mavericks song; the DVD shows dancers acting out each Animal's movements to music and lyrics. You can, however, invent your own music or simply chant the lyrics like a poem, and you can access free Animal videos on the internet. (See especially www.kids.nationalgeographic.com)

● Reading References ●

Cantwell D, Baker L. Psychiatric Developmental Disorders in Children with Communication Disorder. Washington D.C. American Psychiatric Press, Inc.; 1991.

Caplan D. Toward a Psycholinguistic Approach to Acquired Neurogenic Language Disorders. AJSLP Jan, 1993: p 59-83. .

Florance CL, Gazzaniga M. Maverick Mind: A Mother's Story of Solving the Mystery of Her Unreachable, Unteachable, Silent Son. New York, N.Y. Penguin Group Inc., 2004.

Florance CL, Shames GH. Stuttering Treatment: Issues in Transfer and Maintenance. Seminars in Speech, Language, and Hearing. Nov, 1980. Vol.1 No. 4: p 375-388.

Goldstein S, Hinerman, P. Parent's Guide: Language and Behavior Problems in Children. The Neurology, Learning, and Behavior Center.

Grandin T. Thinking in Pictures. And Other Reports from My Life with Autism. New York, N.Y. Random House, 1995.

Ohio Handbook for the Identification, Evaluation, and Placement of Children with Language Problems. Ohio Department of Education. Columbus Ohio; 1991.

Seligman MEP. The Optimistic Child: A Proven Program to Safeguard Children Against Depression and Build Lifelong Resilience. New York, N.Y. Harper Collins Press, 1995.

CPSIA information can be obtained
at www.ICGtesting.com
Printed in the USA
LVIC06n1202111214
418320LV00004B/5